The World's COOLEST Jobs

DRONE OPERATOR

Alix Wood

PowerKiDS
press

New York

Published in 2014 by The Rosen Publishing Group, Inc.
29 East 21st Street, New York, NY 10010

Editor for Alix Wood Books: Eloise Macgregor
Designer: Alix Wood
US Editor: Joshua Shadowens
Researcher: Kevin Wood
Military Consultant: Group Captain MF Baker MA RAF (Retd)
Educational Consultant: Amanda Baker BEd (Hons) PGCDL

Photo Credits: cover image, 1, 4, 5, 6, 10, 11, 12, 14 top and background,
15 top left and right, 16, 17, 18, 19, 20, 21, 25, 28 © Defenseimagery.mil;
7 bottom, 8, 22, 26, 27, 29 © Shutterstock; 9 top and middle, 13 background,
15 bottom © MoD; 9 bottom © public domain; 13 top © Dkroetsch; 13 bottom,
23 © Dreamstime, 24 © John Giles/PA Wire

Library of Congress Cataloging-in-Publication Data

Wood, Alix.
 Drone operator / by Alix Wood.
    pages cm. — (The world's coolest jobs)
 Includes index.
 ISBN 978-1-4777-6023-9 (library) — ISBN 978-1-4777-6024-6 (pbk.) —
 ISBN 978-1-4777-6026-0 (6-pack)
 1. Drone aircraft—Juvenile literature. I. Title.
 TL718.W66 2014
 623.74'69023—dc23
                                    2013027035

Manufactured in the United States of America

CPSIA Compliance Information: Batch #W14PK2: For Further Information contact Rosen Publishing, New York, New York at 1-800-237-9932

Contents

What Is a Drone Operator?

A drone operator flies unmanned aerial vehicles, also called UAVs or drones. The operator flies the drones either from the ground or from another vehicle.

Drones are used by the military, law enforcement agencies, firefighters, and even **conservationists**. They are useful for anyone who needs an eye in the sky. They can be used to relay images or carry and **deploy** weapons.

THAT'S COOL

Unmanned aerial vehicles have been around since 1916. In World War II they were used as targets to train anti-aircraft gunners, and they also flew some attack missions.

UAVs come in many different shapes and sizes.

This IAI Heron UAV is capable of flying for up to 52 hours non-stop.

The use of drones has grown quickly in recent years. They are useful because they can stay in the air for much longer than manned aircraft. A British drone under development has just broken the world record by flying for over 82 hours non-stop! UAVs are much cheaper than military aircraft, and they are flown remotely so there is no danger to the flight crew.

Drone operators on the ground view images from a Heron's cameras during a desert search and rescue training exercise.

FACT FILE

UAVs can be used for:

Target and decoy – simulating enemy aircraft or missiles to provide target practice for their own troops, or to draw enemy fire

Reconnaissance – providing battlefield intelligence

Combat – attacking high-risk locations

Logistics – carrying cargo

Research and development – helping develop new UAV technology

How To Fly a Drone

UAVs can be controlled by a crew many miles (km) away from the aircraft. **Satellites** are used to relay commands to the UAV and to send images back to the operators.

Drone operators describe piloting a Predator aircraft as a little like flying an airplane while looking through a straw! It is quite different from flying an aircraft from the cockpit. Predator pilots have to rely on the onboard cameras to see what is going on around the plane. A typical team consists of four aircraft, a ground control station where the pilots and sensor operators sit, and a satellite link. Around 82 people including support personnel help operate the aircraft. This team can provide 24-hour surveillance within 460 miles (740 km) of the ground control station.

The pilot, left, and sensor operator, right, perform checks after launching a Predator in Iraq. This local crew handle the Predator near the base before handing control to operators in the US who continue its mission.

FACT FILE

The Predator can be programmed to perform simple missions without needing a pilot. For more complex missions its crew consists of one pilot and two sensor operators. The pilot drives the aircraft using a standard **joystick** and controls that transmit commands using a **line-of-sight** data link. When operations are beyond that link's range, a satellite link is used instead. The pilots and crews use the images and **radar** received from the aircraft to make decisions about controlling the plane.

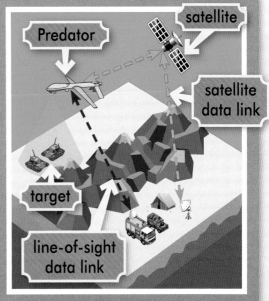

The Predator works much like any small plane. The drive shaft rotates the rear propeller which provides both drive and lift. The remote pilot can alter the angle of the propeller blades to change the height that the plane flies at. A rudder under the propeller steers the aircraft. A power cart is used to start the engine and charge its battery. To stop the engine the operator hits a kill switch located behind one wing.

Military Drone Operators

UAVs are being used more and more for military operations. At present there are not enough trained pilots to fly them as their usefulness has increased so rapidly!

When a military operation is taking place in rough, mountainous **terrain**, it is difficult for the people on the ground to make sure an area is safe. UAVs help search the area and provide armed cover for troops in battle. UAVs also search for roadside bombs and can fire on anyone seen planting them.

👍 THAT'S COOL

UAVs and their pilots are going to be in demand. The US Air Force used to recruit trained pilots for UAV assignments. Now they send some trainee pilots and non-pilots directly to UAV training.

A drone can scan a mountainous area both night and day.

Military UAV operators need many of the same skills that traditional pilots need, including good **motor skills** and excellent vision. They must be able to make decisions under stress and be physically fit. Once chosen for the program, trainees use **simulators** to learn to fly the drones. They learn about the weapons, and the strict rules on when and how to use them. Operators need to learn which locations are friendly and how to positively identify a potential threat.

Drone operators may operate from the battlefield. Here, a British soldier launches a Desert Hawk UAV from a landrover in Afghanistan, which also carries its portable control station.

FACT FILE

Eyesight requirements for drone operators aren't as tough as they are for fighter pilots, but color vision is important. A pilot may need to be able to tell important differences in colors. Some people are color blind. In this image on the right the number 74 should be visible to people with normal color vision. Color blind people will see no number at all, or the number 21, depending on what type of color blindness they have.

The UAVs control station may be located locally, or it can be in another country from the drones it is operating. That can be an odd experience for the drone operator.

In the control station drone operators guide the remotely piloted aircraft. They may be in a trailer in the US while operating on the front line of a war in another country. One of the screens has a live full-motion video feed from the aircraft. A second screen has mission data like the **altitude** of the drone and its fuel level. A third screen displays menus of more data. The drone is steered with a joystick, and pedals control its rudder.

mission data

A pilot and sensor operator on a training mission in a Predator control station simulator.

live video

joystick

The sensor operator controls the camera. He or she can zoom in on the faces of people to assess if they are a danger. A keyboard allows the sensor operator to communicate with intelligence agencies to check if the target is a threat. The sensor operator has radio contact with the command center, which must authorize any use of weapons. A button on the joystick launches the missiles. After an explosion the sensor operator can train the camera on the wreckage to check if the mission was successful.

FACT FILE

The Predator aircraft's **optical** unit is equipped with a targeting system, a TV camera, an **infrared** camera for low light or night conditions, and a color nose camera used by the pilot for flight control. Predators can be equipped with a radar for looking through smoke, clouds, or haze, but lack of use means it is usually removed to reduce weight and conserve fuel. The cameras produce full-motion video and still-frame radar images. The targeting system **laser** allows the pilot to identify targets to be bombed by either other aircraft or its own missiles.

The optical unit underneath a Predator containing the cameras and sensor equipment.

Search and Rescue

UAVs are now routinely used by search and rescue organizations. Their cameras can be used day and night and in bad conditions. **Thermal imaging** cameras can help find missing or injured people by spotting a heat source. Infrared cameras enhance night vision.

Rather than having to land a search aircraft and let the pilots change shifts, the drone can be kept in the air for hours at a time. The Raven is a small hand-launched UAV developed for the US military, but now used for search and rescue too. The Raven can be either remotely controlled from the ground or fly a **pre-programmed** route using GPS navigation. The Raven will return to its launch point simply by pressing a single command button. It can carry color video cameras and an infrared night vision camera and is ideal for searches.

The Raven is launched by throwing it into the air like a model airplane!

Micro UAVs, such as this Aeryon Scout, can be used to search for missing persons. The Aeryon Scout is small, quiet, and easy to operate. It can capture and transmit high quality images and video. It is controlled using a PC tablet, so it can be operated with little training. The operator simply points to an area on the map that they want it to fly to! Its height is controlled by using a scroll on the touch screen. It can be pre-programmed to fly to a series of GPS waypoints.

The Aeryon Scout has a "follow me" feature. It will automatically follow search teams at a set height and distance, giving them a constant view above the search area.

👍 THAT'S COOL

All-weather sensors can providing photographic-like images through clouds, rain or fog, day and night. **Thermographic** images like the one below show any heat source. This can help locate an injured person.

This aerial image was taken by an infrared camera at night. Infrared cameras convert light **photons** into **electrons**, boost them, and then turn them back into visible images.

Spying Drones

Drones are useful at gathering information. They watch and listen without being seen. Some UAVs are small enough to fly through open windows like this nano hummingbird. Others silently watch from the skies.

The Global Hawk drone pictured below is a high altitude UAV. It can survey as much as 40,000 square miles (10,000,000 ha) of terrain a day! A Global Hawk can fly at an altitude of up to 60,000 feet (18.3 km).

👍 **THAT'S COOL**

The CIA's first drone was made using off the shelf technology, such as garage door openers and model airplanes!

A high altitude Global Hawk passing silently high over a mountain range.

FACT FILE

Ideal for special forces missions, the XM156 can be carried in two custom-made backpacks. The total system including the vehicle, control device, and ground support equipment weighs less than 51 pounds (23 kg). The system can hover over an area as well as fly.

XM156

an XM156 and its two backpacks

The British military are using a tiny surveillance drone called the Black Hornet Nano. It is about the size of a pair of sunglasses and has a tiny camera to relay video and photos. It is very light and easy to operate. It can hover and stare, look behind, between, and below obstacles. It sees a useful bird's eye view of situations and places. It is virtually silent and so small that it is almost impossible to spot once it is high enough in the air.

The Black Hornet Nano has been very useful scouting out buildings for the British army.

Drone Operators in the Sky

During the 1960s and 1970s drone operators did get to take to the skies. The DC-130 aircraft was designed to carry Firebee drones and act as the control center.

Operating a drone from a truck cut down a drone's combat range. The drone only had a single, stationary recovery area, too. To improve their range and the ability to recover the drones from anywhere, drone operators took to the skies.

The DC-130 was a type of Hercules, designed for drone control. It could carry four Firebee drones underneath its wings. It could also provide control for up to 16 drones at the same time.

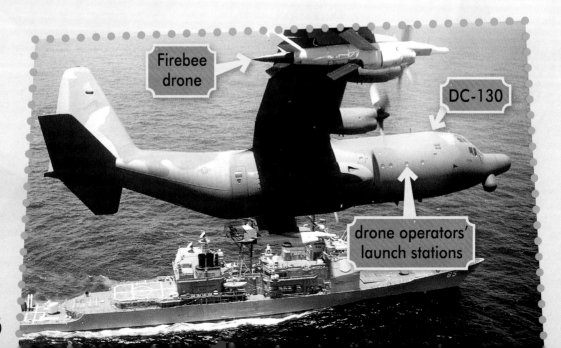

Firebee drone

DC-130

drone operators' launch stations

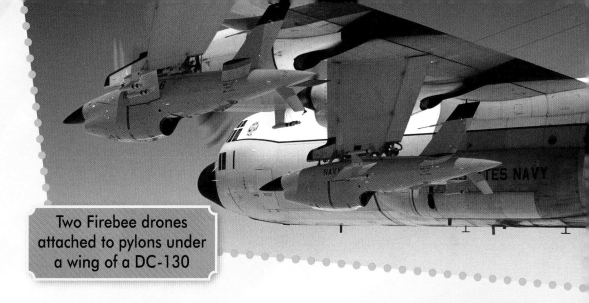

Two Firebee drones attached to pylons under a wing of a DC-130

The drone operators' two-man launch stations on board the DC-130 could launch, control, and track the drones. Instruments displayed data such as the heading, speed, and altitude. A system could show the current position of both the drone and DC-130 on a large map board in front of the operators. The planned track of the drone was drawn on the board, so the crew could immediately spot any change in flight path. The drone controllers also monitored and recorded video data.

FACT FILE

Firebee recovery was the job of the Drone Recovery Officer (DRO) in the control vehicle. The drone was picked up by radar as it neared the recovery area and controlled by the DRO. The Firebee then deployed a parachute, and was snatched out of the air by a waiting recovery helicopter. The drone was pulled up and flown back to base. The Firebee could float for a time, too, if it ditched in water.

More modern Firebee IIs launch from a launch pad.

Drone operators are not just in charge of flying the aircraft. They must be experienced in managing various sensors and weapons, too.

UAVs can carry several different kinds of sensors. A UAV's sensors include cameras, infrared cameras, and radar systems. The UAV can also carry gamma ray sensors which sense a **radiation** threat. Their biological sensors are capable of detecting any airborne biological threat. The chemical sensors analyze the concentrations of each chemical element in the air.

The sensor system or targeting system is fitted here.

An avionics specialist sets up a Reaper's electronic codes.

FACT FILE

Not only can a drone keep watch over a battlefield, it can help fight the battle. Replacing the sensors with a targeting system and loading a UAV, such as a Reaper, with Hellfire missiles transforms it into a fighter. The drone operator has several ways to hit a target. The system can fire a laser or infrared beam. The beam lands on the target and pulses to attract the laser seekers at the end of each Hellfire missile. This process is known as "painting the target." Once a target is painted, the Reaper can unleash its own missiles or other aircraft or ground forces can destroy it.

Hellfire missile

👍 THAT'S COOL

A Predator can carry about 200 pounds (90.72 kg) of weapons. The Reaper can carry 1.5 tons (1.36 t)!

A Reaper waits in a hangar during a sandstorm.

Hellfire missile

One of the more complicated things a drone operator has to do is to launch and to land the aircraft. There are various different methods depending on the type of UAV, where it is based, and where it is needed.

Drones can be launched by hand, using a rocket, using a conventional rolling take off, or by using launch rails. UAVs are even being launched from submarines, by using a canister launched from the trash disposal unit! Once the canister reaches the surface it ejects the UAV into the air. This variety of methods mean a drone operator can launch a UAV from just about anywhere.

An RQ-7B Shadow being catapulted into flight from a rail launcher.

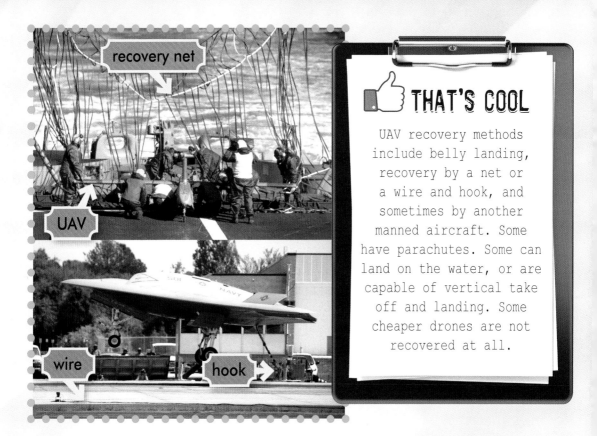

recovery net

UAV

wire

hook

FACT FILE

Sometimes a UAV will be lost. The US Navy have come up with a useful solution, sea lions! Some drones have a pinger that sends out a tone to help the sea lion locate them. The sea lion holds an attachment device in its mouth, on a strong line. Once the line is attached to the UAV, the sea lion tests the connection by pulling it a few times. The sea lion then returns to the boat for a well-deserved reward of fish while the recovery vessel pulls the drone to the surface.

Sea lions help find and recover underwater objects such as UAVs. Sea lions see well in murky underwater conditions.

The Future of Film and TV

Drone operators may soon become a regular part of a film or TV crew. Overhead **panoramic** shots are expensive to get when paying for a pilot's and photographer's time. A low cost drone is a great solution for film makers.

Movie directors often want to use a UAV with a high-definition camera to get panoramic aerial shots or even action close-ups that would be hard to film in the usual ways. Location scouts use unmanned drone aircraft to get great aerial images of locations. Sporting events are being filmed by cameras mounted to UAVs, too. The running costs are cheaper than those for a helicopter. They have low fuel costs, no rental or pilot costs, lower insurance, and no noise concerns. People can learn to fly a simple UAV in a matter of hours. Getting permission to fly a drone in many countries isn't that easy though.

Drones can take interesting aerial shots of sporting events. Their ability to follow the action make them great for sports TV coverage.

THAT'S COOL

Drone filmmaking is relatively easy. A digital camera is mounted onto a UAV. The UAV can be remote controlled or even operated using a smartphone app. Operating a UAV is similar to operating a remote controlled car. Most UAVs also allow users to send their vehicles to GPS coordinates. The video is saved onto the camera to be edited by computer later.

Many smaller UAVs are flown using a handheld controller with a touch screen. The screen displays flight data, including the altitude, heading, bearing, battery voltage, and GPS position.

Some controllers take the aircraft's videostream and display it on a pair of video glasses. These glasses allow the operator to see what the camera is seeing.

UAVs are being used by law enforcement agencies to catch criminals and find missing people. Having an aerial view of a search area is very valuable. The fire service use UAVs to help monitor and combat fires.

British police officers are using drones to tackle crime, anti-social behavior, and even monitor traffic congestion. Their microdrones weigh less than a bag of sugar. They are silent, and can be fitted with night vision cameras. The images they record can be sent back to a control room, police support vehicle, or to an officer on the ground wearing special video glasses.

antenna

video glasses

camera

remote control

👍 THAT'S COOL

UAVs are used to help prevent and detect fires. They can monitor an area both day and night. The UAVs carry various cameras and sensors that provide emergency services with information about the location of any outbreak of fire. Sensors also give firefighters useful information such as wind speed, temperature, and humidity which is helpful for fire suppression.

This photograph taken by a Global Hawk shows an aerial view of wildfires in Northern California. Global Hawk stayed in the air for nearly 24 hours sending detailed images to help manage firefighting efforts.

FACT FILE

The Office of Air and Marine is the world's largest aviation and maritime law enforcement organization. They are part of the US Customs and Border Protection. In this photo, an officer monitors images taken by their UAVs. The surveillance provides border control with information of any illegal activity taking place in remote areas. Drone operators help chase down smugglers and track illegal immigrants trying to cross the border.

A border patrol sensor operator scans the screens

Useful Eye in the Sky

UAVs are useful anywhere people need an eye in the sky. Drone operators can get involved in animal conservation, checking animal populations and looking out for poachers.

👍 THAT'S COOL

Drones are being used for many conservation projects. The Kruger National Park, in South Africa, started using a Seeker II drone to guard against rhino poachers. Anti-whaling activists used an Osprey drone to monitor Japanese whaling ships in the Antarctic.

Elephants are regularly poached for their ivory tusks. Drone operators can help police the area for poachers.

Unmanned aircraft are able to go into areas that may be too dangerous for piloted craft. Drones can be used as hurricane hunters in the air and underwater. UAVs can fly into a hurricane and communicate live data which can be used to monitor its size and strength. UAVs can monitor pressure and temperature and provide more accurate information than manned hurricane hunters could. The UAVs are small and cheap enough to be disposable.

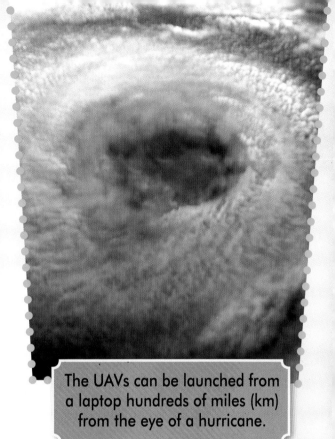

The UAVs can be launched from a laptop hundreds of miles (km) from the eye of a hurricane.

FACT FILE

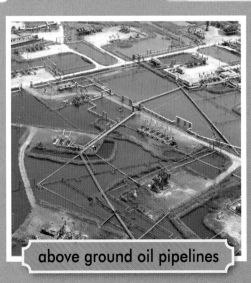

above ground oil pipelines

Oil, gas, and mineral exploration can be performed by drones. Special sensors can sense the strength of the Earth's magnetic field. This can be used to work out which type of rock lies underneath the surface. This knowledge can help experts predict where mineral deposits can be found. The oil and gas industry use drones to monitor above-ground pipelines for damage using digital cameras mounted on UAVs.

Still Want To Be a Drone Operator?

If you are interested in becoming a drone operator it is useful to focus on science and math subjects in school.

Military drone operators have to do military basic training first, and then take advanced specialized training. The advanced training teaches how to perform different types of missions. They learn how to prepare maps, charts, and intelligence reports, how to analyze aerial photographs, and how to use the computer systems.

Military basic training can be tough!

There are some problems to think about when considering the future of drone use. Some people believe that fighting humans with machines controlled from a safe distance lacks the honor that was once a part of warfare. Others feel that if the technology is available, there is a moral duty to use it as it saves pilot's lives. In the civilian world, there is a concern that people's privacy is at risk from being spied on by drones. Life as a drone operator would mean you would have to be happy with how the job dealt with these issues.

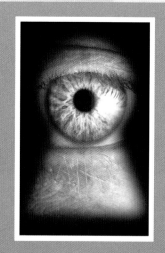

The rise in popularity of UAVs means that many pilots will need to be trained to operate them in the coming years. People who are skilled at playing video games have some of the skills necessary to be drone operators of the future. There is more to being a UAV pilot than just operating the controls, however. Operators have to understand how to fly safely in the airspace. They also need to understand the data the UAVs are receiving and interpret it correctly.

👍 THAT'S COOL

It is helpful to have built and operated remote control vehicles for a career as a drone operator.

Glossary

altitude (AL-tuh-tood)
The height of an object.

conservationists
(kon-sur-VAY-shun-istz)
People who believe in
protecting nature.

deploy (dih-PLOY)
To use or place in position for
some purpose such as battle.

electrons (ih-LEK-tronz)
Elementary particles that have
a negative charge of electricity.

infrared (IN-fruh-red)
Rays like light but lying
outside the visible spectrum
at its red end.

joystick (JOY-stik)
A control lever.

laser (LAY-zer)
A device that generates a
narrow beam of light.

line-of-sight (LYN-UV-SYT)
An unobstructed path
between sending and
receiving antennas.

motor skills
(MOH-tur SKILZ)
Complex movements.

optical (OP-tih-kul)
Relating to vision.

panoramic (pa-nuh-RA-mik)
A full and clear view in
every direction.

photons (FOH-tonz)
Tiny particles or bundles of
electromagnetic radiation.

pre-programmed
(pre-PROH-gramd)
Programmed in advance.

radar (RAY-dar)
A device that sends out radio waves to locate an object by the reflection of the radio waves.

radiation (ray-dee-AY-shun)
Energy radiated in the form of waves or particles.

satellites (SA-tih-lyts)
Objects which orbit the earth.

simulating (SIM-yuh-layt-ing)
To give the appearance or effect of something else.

simulators (SIM-yuh-lay-turz)
Devices that enable the operator to experience events similar to those likely to occur in a real situation.

terrain (tuh-RAYN)
The surface features of an area of land.

thermal imaging
(THER-mul IM-uh-ging)
Using the heat given off by an object to produce an image.

thermographic
(ther-moh-GRA-fik)
An imaging method that uses heat or infrared energy.

👍 WEBSITES

Due to the changing nature of Internet links, PowerKids Press has developed an online list of websites related to the subject of this book. This site is updated regularly. Please use this link to access the list:

www.powerkidslinks.com/wcj/drone

Read More

Burgan, Michael. *Today's U.S. Air Force*. The U.S. Armed Forces. Mankato, MN: Compass Point Books, 2013.

Jackson, Kay. *Military Planes in Action*. Amazing Military Vehicles. New York: PowerKids Press, 2009.

Nagelhout, Ryan. *Drones*. Military Machines. New York: Gareth Stevens Learning Library, 2013.

Index